Lyrical Ballads

Bill Manhire was born in Invercargill, New Zealand, in 1946. He was his country's inaugural Poet Laureate and has won the New Zealand Book Award for Poetry four times. He headed the International Institute of Modern Letters at Victoria University of Wellington, establishing and directing the university's prestigious creative writing programme. His volume of short fiction, *South Pacific*, was published by Carcanet in 1994. His poetry collections include *Lifted* (2007), and his *Collected Poems* (2001) and *Selected Poems* (2014). In 2018, he was made one of the Arts Foundation Icon Artists, an award given to only twenty living artists for their lifetime achievement and contribution to the arts in New Zealand.

Also by Bill Manhire

Poetry collections
Wow (2020)
Some Things to Place in a Coffin (2017)
The Victims of Lightning (2010)
Lifted (2005)
What to Call Your Child (1999)
My Sunshine (1996)
Milky Way Bar (1991)
Good Looks (1982)
How to Take Off Your Clothes at the Picnic (1977)
The Elaboration (1972)

Prose collections
The Stories of Bill Manhire (2015)
Doubtful Sounds: Essays and Interviews (2000)

Collaborations
Tell Me My Name (with Hannah Griffin, Norman Meehan & Peter Peryer, 2017)
These Rough Notes (with Hannah Griffin, Norman Meehan & Anne Noble, 2012)
Dawn/Water (with Andrew Drummond, 1979)
Pine (with Ralph Hotere, 1974, 2005)
Malady (with Ralph Hotere, 1970)

As editor and co-editor
The Best of Best New Zealand Poems (2011)
Are Angels OK?: The Parallel Worlds of New Zealand Writers and Scientists (2006)
The Wide White Page: Writers Imagine Antarctica (2004)
Mutes & Earthquakes: Bill Manhire's Creative Writing Course at Victoria (1997)
100 New Zealand Poems (1993)
Six by Six: Short Stories by New Zealand's Best Writers (1989)
Some Other Country: New Zealand's Best Short Stories (1984, 2008)

Lyrical Ballads

Bill Manhire

CARCANET POETRY

First published in Great Britain in 2026 by
Carcanet
Main Library, The University of Manchester
Oxford Road, Manchester, M13 9PP
www.carcanet.co.uk

Text copyright © Bill Mahire 2026

The right of Bill Manhire to be identified as the author
of this work has been asserted in accordance with the
Copyright, Design and Patents Act of 1988; all rights reserved.
No part of this book may be used or reproduced in any manner
for the purpose of training artificial intelligence technologies or systems.

A CIP catalogue record for this book is
available from the British Library.

ISBN 978 1 80017 544 0

Cover design: Todd Atticus; artwork: Thomas Wright, Plate 16 from *An Original Theory or New Hypothesis of the Universe*, 1750

Printed in Great Britain by SRP Ltd, Exeter, Devon

The publisher acknowledges financial
assistance from Arts Council England.

For Norman Meehan

Contents

1

Come On In	13
Old Poems	14
Country Music	15
Harm	16
Pioneer	18
Lyrical Ballad	19
Yawn	20
Library Song	21
Some Other Words I Think They Sang	22
The Distant Road	23
Getting There	24
The World About Us	25
Domestic Interior	26
Angry Man	27
As We All Know	28
Live Cross	29
Gaza	30
2. The Tobacco Tin	31

3

Stump Speech	61
Too Many Draculas	62
Wonder	63
Signing Off	64
What We Did Before We Walked Away	65
Fancy Dress	66
Picking Up the Dog	68
Learning to Write	69
Hello	70
Cheerful Tom	72
Quite a Lot	73
Cronies	74
Falling Asleep on New Year's Day	75
The 27th of December	76
Mossburn	77
Explaining Dunedin	78
Lecturers	79
Outram	80
Double Honk	81
Friendship	82
Poetry Updates	83
Walter's Fish	84

4. Tell You What   85

Setting Out	119
Hardyesque	120
Without Warning	121
Skara Brae	122
After the Rain	123
The small god is still inventing himself	124
Lonely Way	125
Solstice	126
Poetry Lane	127
Rigid World	128
Sand	129
My Final Poem	130
Late Summer: Waikanae	131
Acknowledgements	133

1

Come On In

We call this room the kissing room
though we have never kissed here.

We enter one by one.
Come on in!

We talk about heartbreak
because we break a lot.

Who is feeling brave today?
Who would like to recite something?

Old Poems

When we were young
we all wrote words on our wrists.

One hand on the other hand,
sometimes someone else's.

Now we tend to run from the carnival.
So many people!

We run and we run till no one.

Country Music

You hurry home, into the open
I've been out there too
never lost a single shoe

never had to say What in the world's
the world coming to

You know there's always someone
standing at a window right here
doing just that, exactly that

head there on the grey pillow
that listens while you sleep

and of course I love the new car
plenty of big varoom
it gives a wee beep when it sees me

Harm

Harm came over the hill
huffing and puffing,
breathless by the time it knocked on the door.

We knew not to answer.
We sang to build courage.
We knew what Harm was here for.

+

All of the songs we sang
were of the old, the terrible war
where blood ran and ran and kept on running.

We sang the chorus of bodies,
the buried and missing, the broken and lost,
and Harm went on knocking

+

and days went by, while Harm held fast –
stones on the roof, against shutters . . .
and Harm hammered again and again

its voice clearer now, too,
the whispering fully grammatical,
names named that we thought we knew

\+

when, suddenly, the noise stopped entirely.
We opened the double-width door
and stepped out into silence.

Nothing in sight.
The rich still beating the poor.
Someone said 'also' then 'furthermore'.

\+

Harm had been done. We were done for.

Pioneer

We need to ford the river.
There's always the other side to consider.
Whether we think about the other side or not,
we need to ford the river.

The boats go on the river
and the river goes on forever.
We need somewhere to come ashore,
a somewhere we haven't been before.

Look over there! A giant flightless bird!
A tree shaped like a pear!
Do we feel fear? We don't. We do?
You know I'll never agree with you.

We like to think we're starting to explore
deep into the far and furthermore.
We use words like hitherto a lot,
we sit by the campfire, watch the clock.

Yet even with the flames, we start to shiver.
We really need to talk.
So many things on which we differ!
When to say whence, when to say whither.

But first of all we need to ford the river.

Lyrical Ballad

I bought a bend in the river. It was a good, quiet bend. You couldn't see around the corner and then after a few steps you could. The water flowed round the bend, which is essentially what you want. Everything else was doing its thing. The Lost Hills were there in the distance. The river was slow as it entered the bend, and maybe just a little faster after that, I don't know why. For a while I wondered about getting a little boat, maybe a raft, but it was walking around the bend that really made me happy. I liked the reliable surprise. It's gone now anyway, that bend, washed away in the last big rains. Now it's just a patch of land: a channel and some structural damage. I suppose I should sell it, but I can't quite make myself. It was everything I ever wanted.

Yawn

His name was Yawn and he came from Iceland.
He started talking about glaciers.
I said, well we have those.
Then it was thermal stuff and bubbling mud.
All that, too, I said. Volcanoes. Ditto.
Waterfalls. Of course.

Then he said, we have no trees, another interesting fact.
We have lots of those, I said. Big forests. Bush.
He said, I don't think you can even see
where you are going with all those trees.

Then he turned on his heel
and vanished into the polar wastes.

Maybe it was Yone, but I will stick with Yawn.
I called after him, words I am still quite proud of:
Well, you can't beat a good diorama!
Whenever I fall asleep, I think of him.

Library Song

The man from the Ministry of Health
has placed my books upon his shelf.
Sometimes he takes one down for me
if I sit where he can see.

He does not read books much himself.

This is a happy time,
especially when the day clouds over.
I hold the book all day, all day,
until the time for reading's over.

His name is Mr Crimson
though the colour of his heart is grey.
I ask him if it is true about his heart
but he says he has not looked and so he cannot say.

He says, The time for reading is over
for the daylight is nearly gone.
This book must now return
to the shelf it rests upon.

The man from the Ministry of Health
has taken my book from me.
He has placed it on the high shelf carefully
with all the other books he has taken away from me.

Some Other Words I Think They Sang

Insects singing in the night.
We were all walking in the same direction.

Be careful. Be strong. Be kind.
That's what they sang.

Sing when the world is worn away.
Some other words I think they sang.

Insects singing in the night.
We were all walking in the same direction.

The Distant Road

Some days I try to stare past
the distant road
at all the roads beyond it

nothing there yet

then the noise of desperate engines
comes on the wind
the sound of waves too and

look!

a child runs into the safe small waves
pauses a moment then
sits down on his well padded

autobiography

Getting There

The man running the roadworks waves us through.
We wave at him as we go, it's easy enough to do,
wave at the man who waves us through.

And then we're at the secret place:
the road becomes the gravel road
becomes the beach.

There's always a track down to the water.
Even when the beach looks empty somebody's on it.
At the moment it's us!

People come round, someone pours a drink.
There's talk of earthquakes, battlefields.
You can't close the gate because it's missing.

The World About Us

There was a weatherboard church
but no settlement to speak of

just a few houses
some bewildered passers-by

I remember wild bells ringing underwater
a line of torn macrocarpas

also the sound of children coughing
someone had made this whole thing happen

Domestic Interior

The willowy blonde
loves trees
of course she does

She walks on the riverbank
beside the trees
and sings her willow song

Now fair and fatal rose the sun
and now began to kill
the many souls on whom it shone
and yet it meant no ill

I heard her voice and its despair
and saw that scribbling on the air

I'm full, says the child
I'm full mummy

Angry Man

He has three barking dogs in the back of the car,
old Silas and . . . I don't know the others.
He has parked the car up over the kerb outside the library
and is standing nearby, waiting to see what will happen.

But nothing happens. He stands there all day
and the dogs fall asleep, and he opens the car door
and now the moon and stars are out in the sky
and here is the light by which his children read their books.

As We All Know

beauty is here barely a moment,
but we still pass it around,
free gift to all. Remembering

now the baby being passed
from hand to hand for what felt like months,
even through a window

twice!

and at last
back to the woman
who never wanted

to let it go.

Live Cross

As I speak to you now, a fine rain is falling.
You can probably just hear the mother calling.

Gaza

The dead boy tries to open his eyes.
He wants to see the world he is leaving.
But there is nothing to see here,
nothing and nothing, and anyway he is gone.
His parents held him while he died
but they are both dead, too.
Or he held them, no one remembers.

2

The Tobacco Tin

The grandfather stole

The grandfather stole the child's first smile.

He wrapped it in tissue paper, and put it inside his old tobacco tin. Later that day, he made his way into the bush, further than he had ever been before.

He buried the tin in a clearing, deeper than anyone could dig. Now the child would always be happy.

That might be Alexander

The phone rang.

Billo said: That might be Alexander. Quick answer it.

Hello, said Nana. Is that Alexander?

A voice said: Hello, I am a giant monkey who likes to ring people up!

Goodbye, said Nana.

Numbers

I was Werewolf 3 in the school play.

I roared seven times, then ran offstage with my arms held out in front of me.

Where I slept

I don't remember where I slept in that house. Every day there were church bells somewhere in the distance, but no churches that anyone could think of. Men came and went, working on Big Hydro and Little Hydro. I remember taking round food, ladling stew out of what felt like a bucket, and later eating with everybody in the huge room where my father sat on his raised platform pretending to read a book whose pages he never turned. At the end of the evening, the men all gone, the dishes and trestle tables cleared away, he would stare at me fiercely and say, 'Now go to your room!', and yes, that must be what I did.

Mongoose

Jarryd said to me: Fuck off. That wasn't very friendly. You fuck off too, I said. What's that, he went, you be careful sonny. I said: I said, you fuck off, Jarryd, I was here first. He loomed up at me. You're looking for trouble, are you little man. Look, just fuck off, I said, or you're a dead fucking mongoose. He looked worried for a moment. He didn't know what a fucking mongoose was. Then he hit me really hard. But then he fucked right off.

The chair

The empty chair in the garden. It is just a chair – with its legs and arms, its strong canvas back. There is moss on it, for it occupies a damp spot far away from the house. No one sits on the chair. There is something a little daunting about it. At dusk it looks like it is made of ancient stone.

One morning I found a handwritten note there: 'My appreciative thanks to all concerned.'

I took the scrap of paper to my uncle, who told me that a homeless man comes and sits in the chair during the dark hours of the night. Now I never go to the bottom of the garden unless it is broad daylight.

Mossy old chair.

When I am in my bed I think about the man out there. I think he is like a king and that for some reason he is terrified like me. He has a large body and dark clothing. He talks to himself. He murmurs and dreams of his kingdom. He has nowhere else to go.

Our History lecturer

Our History lecturer was old and furtive. It was as if he was engaged in some kind of surreptitious wrong-doing. He would write a word on the blackboard – Carthaginians – then step back and glance at it sideways.

Always sideways.

By the end of the lecture hour the board would be covered with words he judged we would find difficult. There were proper names – Justinian, Charlemagne – but also foreign or longer words he enjoyed using – oxymoronic, olla podrida, impresario. Girls sat in the front row, writing them all down.

I only remember one thing he said. 'It's not the facts,' he said. 'It's what we do with the facts.'

After History, we went over to the Botanic Gardens and wandered. There were some high cages you could walk past that had Australian birds in them. Otherwise it was plants and flowers and trees, plus a pond with ducks shitting all over the concrete path around it. It was as if they wanted to stop you reaching the water.

Beyond the Amazon

You don't often see small children at those altitudes, but one came up to me and asked for food. We had none, but I made certain promises, and that is how we came to keep him. We named him Keith. Later, I sat on the bank of quite another river and thought. Indecision is a bad thing, none of us needs it. And: Why has Trudy abandoned me? By then Keith was gone, too. But she was always the phone that shook in my pocket.

Yes, said the cable car driver, I always have two on the go. One book up and the other one down.

After a time

After a time, my writing began to take a new direction. Left after you cross the bridge, and then down what people used to call the stumble-path – steps cut in the bank, occasional big stones – to the water's edge. You go down in daylight and wait till it's dark and there's absolutely no one there. After a while you aren't there either. You feel truly alone, fully neglected. I write all that down – you know, in my head – then start on the difficult climb, no moon, back up to the road. I need badly to return to the house, even though it is empty now, windows open and curtains billowing, still the place where everybody sits up waiting.

Apache

I was just lounging about when Mr Doormat – his real name! – comes up to me. He was the long-time leader of a Shadows cover band. He wanted to tell me how much he despised me. You and your acoustic guitar, he says – I spit on every chord you reach for.

The Famous Painter

I walked into the hospital just behind the famous painter. He had lost a lot of weight and had developed a limp. He was visiting a friend, he said – in fact another painter, one whose life and work had come to nothing, but whom he respected beyond all his peers, and did I know where Ward 27 was? By now I had quite forgotten what I was there for. We counted our way along the corridor: 24, 25, 26. Then he did the big step into space.

Mungo

I called round to see my old friend Mungo (not his real name). Hello Eric, he said (not my real name). Hello, I said and paused significantly. I had made space available, and he stepped into it to tell me that he had spent half his childhood locked in a small room. It did me no harm, he said. No, I said, clearly not. Aside from that and the rumours of war, our conversation went pretty much as usual.

The island

On one side of the island the sea is black; on the other blue. The long causeway accentuates the difference. All the people from the mainland smell of milk.

On the black side, you cast your line into the water and wait, never quite knowing what you will hook. You do not swim there.

The blue side? Well, there are no descriptions of the blue side.

You can go to the far tip of the island, where the great hotels are, and gaze far out to sea, but you will never quite work out where the black becomes the blue. The tourist sand is perfectly white. Sunsets are red. After a storm there are stones that drip with bright green weed.

I had seen things like this

I had seen things like this on the streets of San Francisco, but I was surprised when I bent down to speak to the homeless man, proffering my apple, to hear him whisper: Just remember they are watching you. Well, he was right! There was a whole television crew making a documentary about the writer Frank Sargeson (1903–82), and they felt that some of these 'candid' shots might complement the early stories. We're on the street at all hours of the day and night, said the director. We really need someone with toothache. But can we try that again with a banana?

The old Miskelly bridges

Once there were dozens of bridges along this stretch of river. Occasionally you could see where one had been – wooden posts to which cables had been attached; a coil of tell-tale metal. There was the skeleton of one bridge that must have been in use fairly recently. Its four steel cables still spanned the Miskelly, but the flooring was gone – the cables, like power lines, stretched through empty air.

The Tans' bridge was one of only three that remained. One of the upper cables was thick with black ribbons – one for each of the black Miskelly fish that Mr Tan had caught in his lifetime as a fisherman. He sat out in the middle of the bridge now, seeming to hover above the line that dropped away below him. He was wearing his Stetson hat.

I always approached

I always approached my grandfather cautiously. One time he was sitting in a tent by the river which said, 'This is a relax product.' The tent, that is. My grandfather was rolling a cigarette.

'Never take up this smoking thing,' he said to me. 'It's a filthy habit.' He spat on the ground. 'And try not to spit either. Women don't like it.'

He gave me his old tobacco tin. He said if I opened it, I would be in serious trouble. Of course I did open it, a few days after he died. Just some rather sad old nails.

We felt cold

We felt cold and cruel after the funeral, and we went to bed and slept a lot. The alarm went off and it was the following day, time to stretch and go to work. But I never liked my job, or any of the messages inside the tubes. I didn't like the way my handlebars sloped back. I didn't like hearing about the holiday road toll. They say a man can only break below the surface. Off I went, an overdressed man on a bicycle, already transcribing his journey.

Whenever my grandfather saw me coming

Whenever my grandfather saw me coming, he knelt and called, Alexander! That was never my name – but I always ran to his arms anyway.

The party

Over in the far corner is the man whose wife disappeared when she went for a pedicure. She had saved for months, and the last time anyone saw Iris Croake she was standing on an escalator in a tall building in the mercantile district, rising up to . . . where? Well, we all ask ourselves that now. Croake has written many poems about this moment, all rejected by sympathetic editors, who commonly attach a handwritten note. He keeps referring to 'the whole sorry episode'. None of us want to talk to him.

Shining Cuckoo

But now it is time to visit the Shining Cuckoo rest home, where a man called Eric is always taking off his trousers. When the staff see this, they lead him to his room. Probably they beat him there. Probably he only takes off his trousers to show his bruises. They are black and blue, like bruises in a story. When the staff see this, they lead him to his room. That is how a pattern gets established. His underpants are green. They lead him to his room. Eric, they say, we tell you and tell you. A dog barks in the distance. Yes probably they beat him there.

No one should come to the door dressed like that.

Wonderful world

He used to play piano in hotel lobbies. You could travel, he said, but that was about all the return you got. Some of the bigger chains supplied a dinner jacket. 'People think you look suave and in charge but you're entirely diminished. In the end it's a wonderful world is not so wonderful.' He liked to say things like that. He was always confiding, to anyone who would listen, that this peripatetic existence was almost certainly the reason he never became a published writer.

Daffodil Paddock

There was once a girl called Daffodil Paddock who wanted to be in a Margaret Mahy story. She wrote to Margaret Mahy, who was unfortunately very busy but forwarded her request to Joy Cowley, who sent it on to Jack Lasenby, who likewise etc. etc., well you can probably guess the rest . . . who eventually returned it by special delivery to Mr and Mrs Paddock, who felt very sorry for their poor daughter and passed it on to me, and now – many years later – here she is in my story!

Nana said

Nana said, That is entirely wrong, Alexander. I would always want to talk to a giant monkey who likes to ring people up.

I probably did in fact buy the island.

3

Stump Speech

It's a good day to be getting on a bus
that's going to a suburb you've never heard of.
It's a good day to be on the dark boat that never comes
    to shore.
It's a good day to want to deliver acceptable outcomes
for the whole community. Bear with me please,
I think there should be more of everything.

Too Many Draculas

Too many Draculas are coming down the road.
It's sunset, they're fixing their heads on right.
They need the deep, dark night. They need blood
on their teeth, they're wondering who they'll meet.
Maybe me, maybe you, maybe some brand new Draculas.
Here take this stake, and see how many
you can get. Pick them off one by one. Don't give up yet,
you can always use the cross. Get the slow ones first,
they're often weak from starving. They think
they're ageless, but Jesus take a look!
Anaemic is surely the word that comes to mind.
Their posture is good, but frequently they trip.
That's when you act. Find out where they feed.
Now you can watch whole sections of the city crumple.
So much rubble, so much blood. Also too many Draculas
these days writing poetry: they should stick
to screenplays. Also, too many Draculas getting library cards,
they take out all the books and never bring them back.
And now they're putting pressure on our hospitals.
They flop and lie about, just picking at their food.
They dream all day of secret lairs and lonely paths.
It's always hit or miss. They blow us all a kiss
then promise to unlock an age of economic bliss.
Too many Draculas, too many Draculas,
all climbing up the waiting list.

Wonder

It was the 50th anniversary of my death.
I hadn't expected to last so long.
People came round for a drink,
the way they do. I wasn't there but it was
still the same old house, nice in its way,
with just some nasty new technologies.
I made a few windswept chimney noises
though I realise now there never was a chimney.
I wondered if they wondered what they were listening to.
Anyway, they went on chatting about my poems.
I wonder, one of them said, if anyone wondered
back then whether this stuff made any sense.
Could you even begin to deal with things like that?
You have to remember it was before the rains,
someone said; and another said, you mean before the fires.
I suppose I mean all of it, said the first speaker.
The epidemic, the wars – the whole caboodle. I do wonder
if perhaps he was his own diaspora. All he ever
seemed to find exciting was the moon.

Signing Off

Back when I was leader of the Free World
interplanetary travel was a very big thing.
I went along with it, but always had my reservations.
So many people die along the way, so many bodies
drifting off through space. Imagine! Once upon a time
you could wake up just by opening your eyes.
I wanted to go to the moon, but gladly wrote my songs
    instead.
It mostly worked for me: the dawn was lovely, leaps
    and bounds.
And look over there! Some wild, unsanctioned horses
    going by.
They really like to gallop, I think they want applause.
Yes, I still keep company with incantation. I manage
the odd poem too, though I wouldn't miss it if it went.
For a while, I fancied this might be a sonnet.

What We Did Before We Walked Away

We surrounded the poet with sheets of crumpled paper.
He was dead all right, but now he looked much better.

We abandoned the story about Remington and Underwood
and went straight out to buy the bouncy castle.

The children bounced and said how much they loved us,
we watched them age a little, then a lot.

We noted how the young rats leapt out of the ground:
half-a-dozen gasps of shining water.

You wrote: 'The moonlight shone once more
on the coffin's expensive handles.'

I dispensed with the emergency locator beacon.
Then we told Blind Boy Grunt to change his name.

No no no no no no no, he said.
So we made him change the next one, too.

Fancy Dress

She was the Hanging Gardens of Babylon.
I was drinking behind the bar.

There are six more of me,
she said. Imagine.

Imagine!
It was a bar like any other.

Are you one of the wonders of the world, then?
I heard myself asking this question.

Her hair was wet and romantic.
I was the usual balding man.

She said: Yes, I am.
I have outlived the ancient days

and will continue now for many years to come
as one of the seven wonders of the world.

I checked my phone.
I was waiting to be given a time

for my interview at the Trim Pork Marketing Board.
I think we were both losing interest.

The rain was coming down heavily now.
It had journeyed all the way from the days of yore

with many more tales of desperation
than either of us knew what to do with.

Picking Up the Dog

A railway station in a foreign country.
The trains must cross three borders
before they reach you. All those men
in uniforms! A small dog is running
up and down the platform; it looks hopeful –
I think it must know the one you are waiting for
is worth the trouble.
                        People say you must take
a small gift when you travel. It helps you to arrive.
Likewise when you meet a traveller –
lists of the cities and landscapes you desire,
those you loved and are leaving,
are always of some interest.
Or you can pick up the dog. That will do.

Learning to Write

The man is fixing things but not so well.
He calls on his phone to Ruth
if she could only explain this button
that's entirely new to him.
It doesn't seem to do anything.
It doesn't want to be pushed.
It certainly won't turn. It's just the thing
that life does, is what I hope
Ruth tells him. But she is somewhere in the distance,
possibly Spain or Singapore,
or round the corner in a street off Atlas Street.
The truth is, I'm always looking
for the person and the plot
and most of the words are still beyond me.
I think one of her eyes won't work,
she maybe has a pirate patch,
why not.

Hello

I fell out of someone's
debut novel, and now

I don't know what to do.
It's scary out in the world.

I would like to wake up
in that bed again,

a morning in late
1940s sunlight, just a few

years after the war,
sharing a cigarette

with the woman
who might go on

to be my wife. I don't know,
something must have gone

terribly wrong. I think
maybe the workshop

hated me. I didn't even argue
or run out blindly

into city traffic. It's just
I was never developed.

I stubbed out my cigarette
and then she dumped me.

Cheerful Tom

In my dream Thomas Stearns Eliot
is walking across the Square towards me,
muttering as usual about Pound.
I doff my invisible hat. He chuckles,
I chuckle back. We both know the hat is there
yet we also know it isn't! Life used to be
full of charming problems like this –
don't you think? I'm sure cheerful Tom
agrees.
       Either way, he needs
to get back to his desk, put his grim face on
and get back to work on his poem.
As Pound says, in one of his more cagey emails,
that punch-drunk thing won't change the world
but it might make a few things happen.

Quite a Lot

The desire to tell a story troubles the page
where the poem may or may not turn up.
A character waves, then saddles a horse,
slaps its rump and sends it on its way.
That's probably enough of him.

You know we could live in Italy, or Fiji.
Our cups would all have saucers.
Those men approaching us are rather splendid.
That might also be a thing to say.
It definitely fills the time.

Then the horse came home.
It seemed despondent.
It thinks it never got its apple.
My father used to say *Too true, Thomson.*
He said it more than he needed to.

Far more than he needed to.

Too true, Thomson.
He said it quite a lot.

Cronies

I put a clown in a story once. I was just starting out in the writing trade, and I was a bit lost, like an out-of-work actor haunting the hospital corridors. Of course there's no shame in that – sometimes we all have to freeze in a doorway while the world goes by. Now, at the other end of a long career, I have been considering the viability of an escaped prisoner or, possibly better, a renegade priest. Yes, I agree, we all move on! The renegade priest comes towards me. He wants all my money. Hard to know if this is worth pursuing, and maybe 'money' isn't quite right there. The renegade priest comes towards me. He says he knows where I live. Or does he want my wife? I think I will have to think hard about all this, then ask the group.

Falling Asleep on New Year's Day

The phrase 'Liverpool jacket' drifts into my head
or maybe it was 'She's lost her Liverpool jacket'
one or the other but then I was wide awake again
and writing this poem and wondering about the wiring
of the brain where does it get
its information? I have never been to Liverpool
well just the once to catch a ferry to Dublin
which may or may not count
I would say it didn't
I have no idea what a Liverpool jacket
might or might not look like
maybe some sort of windcheater who knows
not even a colour but possibly stripes
maybe not even an item of clothing
and I was only passing through
though at least it's out in the world now
the Liverpool jacket that was there in my brain for a bit
maybe worn by John Paul George and Ringo
though I very much doubt it
and certainly not here in Waikanae
where I have already lost it

The 27th of December

27 December, 1954. Tired tinsel.
Angels exhausted by the summer heat.
Also my birthday. The boys
from the Rabbit Board are loading their guns,
there's work to do. They gave me a smoke
to smoke behind the hen-house – sort of
a present. No internet back then, just comics.

I went just now to one of those birthday
sites on the web, and it says: 'The people
born on this day are less famous
than people born on other days.'
So that was a very good move for Jesus,
coming along on December 25.
Two days later, he'd have been nobody.

Mossburn

The talkative words are heading off to school.
The teacher doesn't like them.

They make us happy though
up here in the trees
and the birds don't mind

and we were poor back then –
we licked the flavour off the plates.

Explaining Dunedin

In Dunedin we lived
between the station and the stars.
Yes I mean the railway station.
The world back then was pure right now,
grey and shining and pretty much improbable.
We counted the sides of the Octagon
yet somehow always came up short.
We wandered away down Stuart Street
where my mother was still scrubbing
the doorstep to the city – yes someone
has to do these things. One day
she will find her cottage by the stream,
but not this morning. Early drinkers
were at work already, wiping
their broken boots, yelling a lot to fill the void.
They wanted to discuss their secret lives.
So long ago – and yet right now.
I guess there's a lesson here for all of us.
I'm looking for it even as we speak.

Lecturers

They're all gone now,
the good and the bad . . .

some who mainly got by
by reading their words aloud

and others who made you want
to open a book, and then another book forever.

I think the bad ones loved the things
they taught but mostly couldn't show it.

Maybe you just stop learning,
then one day, ta-da, you're a teacher?

You look around the room
in which no one opens their mouth.

The world begins to drone.
You're on your own.

Outram

My name is Bobby Outram, and I live in a little place called Outram, out on the Taieri Plain. Go up the hill from Outram and you're pretty soon in what I call stone country. I went up there one day recently and this thing happened that I'm going to tell you about now.

I pulled the car over to the side of the road, as I had spotted a mysterious large animal patiently waiting by a rocky outcrop. I was intrigued.

It turned out to be, of all things, a pantomime cow.

The two women inside it were stunningly beautiful. I realised I could not choose between them. So back I came to Outram, where I have lived to this day.

Yes, Bobby Outram from Outram. You can get good coffee here.

Double Honk

My annoying friend no longer has the energy to be a pain in the neck. He is tired. When he gets to his feet to go home, he looks exhausted. We have known each other for years and he has always annoyed me. Yet now I am beginning to feel sorry for him. I wish I did not find him so annoying, I wish I were a more generous person. My poor friend can barely get into his car. Now he gives a chirpy double honk on the horn. This is typical. Not the honk so much as the double honk. I will be glad to see the back of him.

Friendship

We like to be alive.
We want to be doing better. We do!
We leave the house and drive to another house.
Yes, it's true, you can travel by car right across our city.
It takes all day, like some medieval quest movie,
and there are many tests and dangers
but, eventually, there they are, Dougal and Misty,
not to mention the new baby, whose name still escapes me.
Kisses all round! And now alas already it is time to go.
Well, we are determined people!
We like to be home in time for breakfast.

Poetry Updates

Yes, there will be sadness.
There will be metaphors and music.
There will be music and the lovely names.

There will be the beating of hearts,
the happiness of trees beside water,
plus death with its aches and gratitude.

And more on this throughout the day
as fresh information comes to hand.

Walter's Fish

How am I doing?
ruined roads and flooded paddocks
again and again and again
oh can't complain

roof ripped off but got the tarp
and help is coming it's mostly a waiting game
as for the health oh much the same

yes it's all a bit of a pain
no, can't complain

anyway, would you like to have this fish

4
Tell You What

'Who is it that can tell me who I am?'
King Lear

Back Country

Between Every Street and Intermediate Street
there's a map. You can walk barefoot across it
and never leave New Zealand. Trees come and go,
I've sometimes seen a river. One day I knocked on a door
but no one answered. Hello, I called, softly, and again
just a bit louder, then nudged my way in. No one.
1950s wallpaper, with baggy scrim behind it.
A photograph of the farm on Rugby Road.
It used to go all the way to Invercargill.

Geography

Eons ago our earth was flat. Literally and actually flat. That's why these days, years after the planet grew geologically round, a few people still hold to the old belief. All those big brains in the universities, historians and so on, and they can't even begin to see it. Well it's always a battle for the hearts and minds. Over in Australia they're mostly very badly brought up. Also, much of Japan is built on reclaimed land. That's why the Japanese people are masked and mysterious. They like to cling to their secrets.

At the Easel

I have finished painting Sunset Over the Offal Pit.
I didn't much enjoy working on it.
It needed so much detail that eventually had to vanish.
All those bits of bodies. The air that was not fresh.

A Consultation

I was born on horseback
at the edge of the battlefield
and yes it's a hard life

hard work climbing the stairs
to the room where the doctor
puts this peg on your finger

then a thing round your arm
and a sort of pumping then a sigh so no
not a place you want to linger

it's always good to get back
to the trees and the clouds
and the hills and the hawks and the horses

Dusk

It's got me beat, the way
the hills just fall asleep.

Complaints

Somewhere in my head I can see
a bored girl sitting at a desk
and there's this big, big queue
stretching right out to the edge of town.
Occasionally she calls out Next
but no one goes home happy.
Look I could probably do the job myself,
even though I'm not at my best.
Next, please. Next, please. Next!

Dark City

The city is made of its own glow.
That's how we know it's a city.

A million people come and go,
and that also helps us.

But, look, I don't really know,
it's primarily the glow.

Bygone

It's odd isn't it, how one day these days
will end up being the old days.

Let bygones be bygones.
Well I know that's probably not the phrase.

But it's a thing I think about more and more.
We're living in the days of yore!

I Know Best

I think October is the month with the most beautiful name.
There are no other real contenders.
I have looked at April, and of course at May and June,
and there are many fine women who share these names.
I also have a lot of time for July.
But I think I will stick with my original position.

The Prime Minister

He thinks he's got all the answers
but we'll see about that.

I Don't Even Eat Apples

People of all sorts love the moon,
or so says a man on the radio.

But I could easily have told him that.
It's beautiful and out of reach,

and sometimes we look up high
and can't even find it.

I still put it in my paintings
and it will certainly be there

in some of the new ones.
It makes us all feel a little strange

yet properly human,
mysterious as that apple core over there

on the back step, now where
on earth did that come from.

Looking Back

Yes, played a bit though I never liked the up-and-under.
So many ways in which you can blunder.

+

They want to sympathise and understand.
But all you want really
is someone who'll give you a bit of a hand.

+

You know I used to be married, I graced the marriage bed.
You can feel a bit helpless, heading back
to all those places in your head.

+

The trouble is something's ripping out my memory.
Every day they take a wee bit more.
But what for?

+

No I can't get up not at the moment
but that doesn't get me down.

+

I still like to go for a run in the car.
You have to claw something back!

The moon, the snow, the evening star,
one or two friends who still say There you are.

+

Anyway.
Bring back the Great Benyon, that's what I say.

+

Now he could make a lady vanish.

Breakneck Speed

They say that's what he was going at.
Not much use to the rest of us
back here still trying to measure the distance
between a boy and a body.

You Don't See Ditches Much These Days

do you

Tell You What

One bird explains the sky to another.
That's the way they operate.

+

In the 1950s all the boys had big ears.
Those were embarrassing years.

+

Every boy with his book.
Every sheep with its showground.

+

We used to call the stove the range.
I don't see why that should have had to change.

+

Raewyn keeps in touch.
I never liked her much.

Whatever They Are

After the colonoscopy
there's a BLT and a flat white.

I could also do with a deckchair.
No, make that a beanbag!

Raewyn's Sister

Always a new boyfriend with that one.

Missing

The names for clouds.

For the Auckland cousins.

All the bits of a church.

The End of the World

Some people think the end of the world is coming,
they think they know everything but they don't.
Yesterday I got a thing in the mail
that says hundreds of gorgeous women
are waiting to chat with me.
I don't think I'll bother this time round.
The electric toaster keeps me going,
it can do six pieces at once.

Loose Change

I still remember that.

A Final Warning

I walked past the stars
the silence of grandfathers

I was going somewhere but where

I went left at first then right
then way off course then back to somewhere

near the middle
did this mean I was ready to die

well they've been testing me for everything
I think I've got the lot

Always in the Sin Bin

There is only the first time.

Nothing comes again.

The wrong person is waking me up.

The wrong one is walking out the door.

Phone Call

No, no one's suggested pulling the plug,
though sometimes they joke about it.

No, plenty of people are taking an interest.

Raewyn was asking about the girls up in Ashburton
plus one or two of the others.

Yes, she's good like that.

Well, there's always a bit of an uproar
down the far end of the corridor.

You Know

if you fall over in the shower
well they have a cord for that
you can go ahead and pull it
they think of everything these people

Bit of a Problem

Too exhausted by coughing
to go on coughing

Curtains

They'd like to switch me off
at the wall. It doesn't mean a thing.

People sit beside me when I sing.

Hamlet

The ghost enters, licking its lips.
Yes, that's it: the show's over.

5

Setting Out

Here comes dawn, bringing back the light.
Everywhere it's quiet.

Where shall we go?
Spring is fine but autumn is here at the window.

Hardyesque

What's that at the window,
hitting against the windowpane?

The weather, Maureen, I hate it.
Weather and war. Those twain.

Then what?
Then more and more of the same.

And later on, more rain, Maureen.
More rain.

Without Warning

Ancient guitar
with just three
strings

& now since I picked
you up in lockdown
only the one

I want you to know
you still make me
think of Sappho

Skara Brae

Birch, hazel, willow.
And beside these someone
must once have placed her pillow.

After the Rain

we climb out
on to the roof

& tiptoe right
to the edge

we want to see
where the water

shakes its wings

The small god is still inventing himself

Last week scarlet & pale
then just a hint of blue

always changing
always a little overdue

yesterday he was apples
today mostly apples

Lonely Way

Between the gallery and the actual temple
is a path called Lonely Way.
We walk there most weekends.

Sometimes a small boy runs past us . . .
not even noticing we are there.

This makes us sad in the evenings.
He used to come often to our house.

Solstice

a month of snow
the desperate birds

hello
to the lantern
hello to the hiding one

+

hello

Poetry Lane

It leads down to the river
where you can sit all day imagining
the slow walk home.

Rigid World

beyond the little villages

another gathering of canals and bridges

songs stung by images

a swarm of midges

softening rigid world

darkness approaching in feet and inches

Sand

always comes home
from the beach

the little children reach and reach
for the last life in the day

and then it is slow dusk
a hose on the lawn

the runner beans running up
into the sky

like a story, like something read
to help us sleep and yet

we are asleep already

My Final Poem

Someone rides a bicycle through a cemetery,
then in and out of my poem.
Why would anyone do that?

I was expecting a dark horseman,
not a clown on a bicycle.

Late Summer: Waikanae

People like watching the dusk.
A father likes saying you must,
you mustn't, you must.

A dog runs along the sunset beach.
It isn't chasing anything.

Acknowledgements

Many thanks to the editors of the following publications and platforms, where a number of these poems first appeared: *A Fine Line*, *The Anchorstone Press*, *Bad Lilies*, *Broadsheet*, *The Hopkins Review*, *Landfall*, *NZ Poetry Shelf*, *North & South*, *PN Review*, *Poetry Birmingham*, *Poetry Ireland Review*, *Poto*, *Roll Your Own Books* and *Stress Test*.

Very particular thanks to Fergus Barrowman, Ashleigh Young and Caoimhe McKeogh at Te Herenga Waka University Press, and to John McAuliffe and Michael Schmidt at Carcanet, for many moments of encouragement, wisdom and rescue.